See
Dick and Jane
Start a Homebased
Business

How to Life the Life You Want and
Spend More Time With Your Family by
Working From Home!

Jeanne Gormick

See Dick and Jane Start a Homebased Business
How to Life the Life You Want and Spend More Time With Your
Family by Working From Home!

Gormick's All American Publications
Laguna Niguel, CA
(949) 534-2180
www.jeannegormick.com

www.jeannegormick.com
jeannegormick@gmail.com

ISBN 978-1-7344154-1-4

Cover Design: Chris Williams

10 9 8 7 6 5 4 3 2
First Edition, 1995

Printed in the United States of America

Contents

Introduction

I sincerely hope that you find this resource valuable and helpful in your quest for the freedom and financial success that owning a homebased business can provide.

I want to help you…

Jeanne

Contact me today!

jeannegormick@gmail.com

Chapter 1:
See Dick and Jane Do
Their Homework

Dick and Jane want to sell Widgets.

See Jane file the "fictitious name statement."
See Dick call the city to get the business license.

Dick and Jane are married. They decide to run
their business as sole proprietors.

They want to save money, so they will use a home
office.

See Dick and Jane be very up-to-date. They will
be homebased business owners.

See Dick and Jane talk to their insurance
professional about liability insurance and get a
rider on their homeowner policy to cover the
business equipment.

See Dick and Jane talk to their tax, legal and banking professionals.

See Dick and Jane do everything the right way. They are Widget professionals.
See Dick and Jane write down their goals. If they don't have goals, they won't know where they are going. They need to know where they are going.

See Jane's friend, Zeke, tell them they need to create a "**vision statement**" and a "**mission statement**" to know what goals to have.

See Dick and Jane sit down.

See Dick and Jane talk.

See Dick and Jane think about their family.

See Dick and Jane decide important business goals to make their family better.

See Dick and Jane discover their **vision**. See them write it down.

See Dick get a book to help them understand a business plan. See Dick and Jane have a written business plan.

Chapter 2:
Now Dick and Jane
Need Customers

See Jane go to Google.

See Dick ask potential clients what they need. See Jane ask her business friends for help.

Now, they are ready to tell people they have the best Widgets in town.

Dick and Jane must name their Widget product or service.

They want to sell Widgets for a very long time. They must think "**long term**," when they name their business.

See Dick and Jane pick a name that will grow with all their Widget sales.

See Dick and Jane pick a name that is unique and easy to recognize.

See people play with Widgets. See people have fun with Widgets.
See Dick and Jane call their Widgets, "Widgets".
See the funny name for a funny product. See the name **"fit"** their Widgets.

Chapter 3:
See Poor Dick and Jane –
See Them Discover That Not Everyone
Needs Their Widgets

Dick and Jane must identify their **"target market"**.

See Jane's friend, Sally, tell them to ask lots of questions about who needs to buy their Widgets.

- Who will buy Widgets?
- What geographic area can they service?
- Are there other companies selling the same Widgets?
- What makes Dick and Jane's Widgets special?

See Dick and Jane get discouraged.

See Sally and Zeke help Dick and Jane get through the tough times. That's what friends are for. Sally and Zeke are Dick and Jane's "**mentors**" for the tough times.

Now, see Dick and Jane begin to understand about their target market.

Zeke says the target market is important for "**advertising**," as well as "**marketing**". See Zeke give them more questions to ask about their "**target audience**"...

- What do they read?
- What radio or TV stations do they listen to and when?
- Where do they go for business and recreation?
- Where do they shop for Widgets?
- How do they make their final selection (convenience, cost, location, etc.)?

Chapter 4:
See Widgets Get a "Logo" and "Packaging"

Dick and Jane have done their **"market research."** See Dick and Jane understand their target market.

See the logo appeal to their target market. It must be remembered easily. People will see the logo and know it is a genuine Widget.

See Dick and Jane hire a good designer for their logo, packaging, brochure or business card.

See them find someone who will work well with them. See them find someone who understands (and likes) Widgets.

See Dick and Jane look at many samples many designers have done for many clients.

See them pick another homebased professional.

See this talented designer understand what they need.

She is not too expensive.
See Dick and Jane like their new logo and packaging.

See Dick and Jane put their new logo on all the Widget "**marketing material**".

Chapter 5:
See Dick and Jane Market
Their Widgets

Dick and Jane have only a little bit of money left.

They need the highest quality marketing materials possible, but maybe a website is better to start with.

And See Jane get business cards on nice "card stock" from a nice printer.

The Widget business is fun.

See Dick and Jane's business cards are fun to look at.

If Dick and Jane were stuffy old CPA's, they would have to have stuffy, old business cards.

The nice printer told them the card should match their type of business.

See the nice printer make sure the cards match the Widgets letterhead and envelopes, website, email and their social media. See everything has the Widget logo on it. See the same color and font.

See Dick and Jane's phone number, fax number, website and e-mail contact information on the business cards. See Dick and Jane's names and titles on the cards.

See how big and important Dick and Jane look.

The cards say that Dick and Jane & Associates sell Widgets. Now, everyone will know what they do.

Dick and Jane want to be different. They want their business cards to stand out. See Dick and Jane use the back of the cards to put their "**client profile**." (See **Dick and Jane Get Referrals**)

See them take the business cards everywhere, even on vacations.

Everyone needs good Widgets!

Everyone will love their Widgets.

Business cards are not expensive. See Dick and Jane still have a little money left, but they need to save up to get good quality brochures. Business cards are a good start, but they can use the many tools available to create their own brochures. They don't need to hire a professional for that!

Chapter 6:
See Dick and Jane
Learn to Network

See Jane's friend, Sally, say to join an association to "network" with other business professionals.

Networking is really good for homebased professionals. Sally says the Chamber of Commerce is good for meeting many people.

Many people there need Widgets.

Sally says to go and visit many chambers of commerce and other groups before joining.

Jane must see which is best for selling Widgets. The group must have members who match their "target audience." See Jane save time and money.

Chambers of commerce "facilitate" networking. There are name tags. They let you pass around business cards. They give you time for "30-second commercials" or "elevator speeches."

These are for "self-introduction."

Chamber "mixers" bring people together to talk about business. That's what networking is.

See Sally invite Jane to the next mixer.

Sally says that networking is more than getting new customers and creating relationships...

- See Dick and Jane establish a business support system.

- See Dick and Jane get important business information.

- See Dick and Jane trade Widgets for other products and services.

- See Dick and Jane save lots of money.

See Jane get to the mixer early to meet all the other business people.

See Jane get her coffee and go to meet people.

See Jane meet lots of people.

See Jane ask everyone what they do (before she tells them what she does.) People like to talk about their businesses.

People like Jane, because she listens to them. She has learned to listen.
See people tell her why they need to buy Widgets as Jane listens to them. This makes selling easy.

See everyone like Dick and Jane, because they listen with interest.

See Jane take her food to the table. See Jane eat **after** she has met lots of people.

Jane does not waste time.

See Sally tell Jane to sit where people will see her, when she stands up.

Jane has practiced her 30-second commercial.

She is ready. See Jane stand up.

See Jane say, "I am Jane with Dick and Jane & Associates. Do you want to look better in business? We can help. We sell Widgets, the best Widgets available and they don't cost a lot of money. Widgets will improve your business image. I am Jane with Dick and Jane & Associates."

See Jane do a good job.

See people come to ask Jane all about her Widgets.

See Dick's friend, Zeke, suggest a business club.

Zeke is not a homebased business owner. See the business club meet at Zeke's facility.

This is good for Zeke's business.

See Dick go to the business club.

Dick is the only one who sells Widgets. Business clubs are like that. They only let one kind of each business come to the meetings.

Widgets are the best widgets at the best price.

See Dick sell lots of Widgets.

See Dick and Jane collect everybody's business card and give everybody their business card.

See Sally remind them that they are not building card collections. They are building "**business relationships**".

See Sally tell them to label the back of the cards with the date and location when they met the person. See Sally remind them to record special notes about the person and why they might need Widgets, too.

See Dick and Jane use a business card app on their phones, so they will always be able to find their potential customers.

See Dick and Jane put the information into their computer.

Sally doesn't have a computer or a phone app yet. See Sally copy all the cards on a copier and put them in a notebook, so she can find everybody she meets.

See Dick and Jane sit down.

See Dick and Jane decide which groups are best.

See Dick and Jane consider...

- Location
- Cost (fees and fines)
- Make-up and size of group

- Personality of group

See Dick pick a service club. See Dick join the business club. See Dick and Jane join the chamber of commerce.

Jane is in the PTA. Dick and Jane go to church. They go to the gym.

See people come to ask Jane all about her Widgets.

See Jane play tennis at the tennis club. See Dick play golf at the country club.

See Dick and Jane network with everyone, everywhere. See them tell **everyone** about their Widgets.

People like people who get involved. See Dick and Jane get involved.

See Jane become an active chamber volunteer.

See Dick serve as treasurer for his new business club.

Dick and Jane go to every available seminar and workshop to learn how to sell Widgets.

See Dick and Jane share business cards with other people selling things.

See many people need Widgets.

See many people like their Widgets.

See many people buy their Widgets.

See Dick and Jane talk to people they don't know.

See Dick and Jane talk business.

See Dick and Jane be careful not to socialize too much. They can socialize at church and playing sports, but see Dick and Jane focus on selling Widgets.

Chapter 7:
See Dick and Jane Learn
All About Referrals

Do you remember when Sally told Dick and Jane to build relationships, not card collections?

Relationships can lead to customers in two ways.

First, people buy from Dick and Jane, because they like them.

There are many Widgets. Widgets are pretty good, but there are many good Widgets.

See Dick and Jane sell many Widgets because customers like them.

See Sally tell Dick and Jane about "**referrals**."

See Sally explain that customers who like Dick and Jane will want to help them.

Do you remember when Dick and Jane put their "client profile" on the back of their business cards?

See the client profile list all the people who can benefit from having their very own Widget.

That's how Dick and Jane can tell other satisfied customers the best people to help them make their Widget business grow.

Good customers want to help Dick and Jane with their Widget sales.

Dick and Jane will help them build their businesses, too.

See them become **"referral partners."**

See Sally help Dick and Jane make their client profile list.

Dick and Jane are surprised at how many people can use Widgets. Sally says their customers will be surprised, too.

See Jane figure out that maybe they should focus on some specific professions that use Widgets the most.

See Sally get Dick and Jane thinking about many possibilities.

See Dick think about how to tell their satisfied customers about their client profile.

See Dick and Jane help their "Referral Partners" grow their businesses.

See Dick and Jane's business grow, because they help others. See it grow big. See it grow very, very big.

Chapter 8:
See Dick and Jane Become Famous

See Zeke tell Jane to get **"good press."**

See Dick and Jane decide to hold a grand opening.

See Dick call the paper. See Dick ask who should receive the release.

See Jane go to the library.

See Jane learn to write a double-spaced, simply written **press or email release**.

See the press release answer the questions "who, what, when and why."

See Dick and Jane have pictures made of them with their Widgets. (See Dick use the pictures in the brochure, too.)

See Dick send the release and their pictures to the local paper and the Chamber of Commerce he has just joined.

See Dick and Jane distribute flyers everywhere. The local paper comes out to take pictures.

The Chamber of Commerce announces the grand opening in its newsletter.

See Zeke teach Dick and Jane to send a press release for everything.

Jane is in the PTA. She is selling tickets for their talent show.

See Jane volunteer to be the contact person.

See Jane submit a press release and her picture to the local papers.

See Jane's name, number and business listed in the article about the talent show.

People will see Jane's name and face. See the people remember.

See people remember Widgets, too.

Now lots of people know Dick and Jane sell Widgets.

Dick and Jane like to be famous. It is good for their business.

See Dick and Jane develop a "**PR campaign.**"

They look at their year and make their plans.

See Dick and Jane decide when they will send press releases all through the year.

See Dick and Jane remember next year's first anniversary of Widgets.

See Jane remember she will be the PTA President in September.

See Dick plan to send a release for the Homebased Business Week Celebration.

See Jane remember to announce next season's new line of Widgets.

See Zeke remind them to send thank-you notes to the editors and reporters for doing feature stories on them.

Chapter 9:
See Dick and Jane Build
Relationships and Become
Famous Speakers

See Zeke tell Dick the secrets of **"public speaking"** to build his business and get **"free press"**.

Zeke likes to talk to big groups of people about how his business can help them (remember **benefits**).

See Zeke build relationships with many people by speaking to them.

See Zeke tell Dick about his Toastmasters International, Inc. Club.

See Zeke "host" the Toastmasters Club at his facility. This is good for Zeke's business.

See Dick go to a Toastmasters meeting.

- See Dick join Toastmasters.
- See Dick learn to make audience eye contact.
- See Dick speak properly.
- See Dick inspire his audiences.
- See Dick use good visual aids.
- See Dick gain speaking confidence.

See public speaking expand Dick's 30-second commercial. See his 30-second commercial become a speech.

See Dick talk for twenty minutes about how Widgets can change people's lives. See Dick be careful not to over sell Widgets. See Dick "**educate his audience**." See many people come up to Dick to ask about his Widgets.

See Dick become a "**recognized widget authority**."

See Dick appear in the paper and on the Internet as the speaker at the local chamber of commerce meeting. See Dick get more good press.

See Dick join a "**speakers' bureau**".

See Dick do lots and lots of speaking.

See Dick ask for "**letters of recognition**" from his best times speaking.

See Dick use these to get more "**speaking engagements**".

See Dick use these letters in his marketing materials.

See Dick get paid for speaking **and** selling Widgets!

See Dick conduct Widget "**seminars and workshops**".

See Dick become big and famous selling Widgets.

Chapter 10:
Oh, No! See Dick and Jane Send Junk Emails

Not really...

See Dick's long list of people he has met at mixers, in his business club, at company open houses, at the grand opening, at speaking engagements and other meetings. Jane has met people, too. They are people who might buy Widgets (**target audience**).

See Dick and Jane decide to send just to those who will remember them, but they always include an **"unsubscribe" option**.

They have sold many Widgets over the last 3 months.

See Dick and Jane have enough money to spend on a nice brochure.

Dick and Jane sell Widgets better than anyone else, but they do not write good words or make pretty pictures.

See Dick and Jane learn **"when to hire professionals"**.

See Dick and Jane hire a writer, a graphic designer and a printer to create a nice brochure for them to send.

See the business writer write the text.

See the graphic designer add pretty pictures.

See the printer print their new brochure.

See Dick and Jane's new Widget brochure.

See Dick and Jane send their new brochure to their target audience.

See Sally remind them to make **follow-up calls**.

See Zeke tell them about a free listing in a directory going out to all area residents. These people are not all in their target market, but the cost is right. See someone who might know someone else who needs their Widgets.

Chapter 11:
See Dick and Jane
Develop a Marketing Plan

See Zeke encourage them to keep going. See Sally remind them that someday they will be successful - very, very successful.

See Zeke advise them to create a written **"marketing plan"** just like their business plan.

See Zeke tell Dick and Jane to look over the target market and target audience questions from before.

See Dick and Jane decide what might work for their own Widget business...

- Send Letters with brochures (**Direct Mail**)
- Write and Submit Articles About Widgets
    - Trade Publications
    - Local Papers
    - Local Magazines

- Blogs
  - Send Press Releases
  - Advertise
    - Newspapers
    - Magazines
    - Radio/TV
    - Association Newsletters
    - Catalogues
    - Offer Coupons
    - Craig's List
    - Specialty Advertising
    - Signs
    - Leverage Social Media
    - Use Google Adwords
    - Hire a Professional to Help With SEO
  - Attend Meetings
  - Support Nonprofit Causes
  - Become A Public Speaker
    - Join Toastmasters to Practice Speaking

See Dick and Jane have lots of choices. See Dick and Jane have too many choices!

See Dick and Jane look at their budget and decide what to try first. See Dick and Jane put a time limit on trying different things to see what works the best.

See Dick and Jane plan to send a Widget Wonders **"email newsletter"** as soon as they have enough money.
Clients and prospects need to know new ways to use their Widgets. Dick and Jane will include advances in Widget technology and other industry trends in their email newsletter and on their blog.

Dick and Jane don't have much extra money left right now, but see them buy Michael Daehn's Internet Marketing for Newbies on Amazon for more ideas.

See Dick and Jane become sad that so much money goes back into their Widget business.

See Sally tell Dick and Jane it is "OK".

See Sally explain, "There are many expenses in starting a business."

Dick and Jane need to advertise, but don't know where to go.

See Sally suggest they look at places where other people selling Widgets (**the competition**) advertise consistently.

See Dick and Jane find that advice helpful, but they can't advertise everywhere they want to. They don't have enough money.

See Dick and Jane get frustrated.

Chapter 12:
See Dick and Jane Advertise

See Dick and Jane start to research advertising possibilities.

Do they use the Internet "pay for clicks" ads? How and which ones? Do they advertise in magazines or newspapers? Do they go to the county-wide paper or the little community paper? Radio or TV advertising? Do they distribute flyers? Where? Do they use coupons? Do they put their name on a give-away product ("**specialty advertising**")? Do they put a sign on their car? Do they buy a space on the grocery cart? Do they put a sign up at the bus stop? Do they buy a sign on the bus? (**Note:** Homebased businesses usually cannot put signs in their front yard or on their roofs. The neighbors would get mad.)

See Dick and Jane get <u>so</u> confused.

See Dick and Jane go to Zeke and Sally for help.

See Zeke and Sally help.

See Zeke and Sally help Dick and Jane watch to see where other Widget sellers (**the competition**) advertise. If they use the big county paper every weekend, Dick and Jane should try that too. If they advertise in the Google search ads, Dick and Jane should do that too.

See Dick and Jane follow their competition onto Facebook, You Tube, Instagram and not so much Twitter. See Dick and Jane place a bigger, better ad.

See Dick and Jane listen to the advertising professional.

See the advertising professional tell them they need to provide potential Widget buyers with 27 **"impressions"** before they begin to recognize Widgets. The advertising professional is not just trying to spend their money.

See Dick and Jane trust the advertising professional.

See Sally tell Dick and Jane another secret.

Sally says to buy ad space in the paper or a magazine and make it look like an article. This is called an "**advertorial**." That will give them the "**credibility**" of an article and the guarantee that it will appear. A press release is free, but it might not appear in the paper. Paid for ad space always appears.

See many people read about Widgets.

Zeke likes using specialty advertising, because the product has his business name on it and lasts a long time.

See Dick and Jane use specialty advertising to get in their client's face every day.

See Dick and Jane receive many calls for Widget.

See Sally tell Dick and Jane to experiment with different things to see what works.

Sally likes coupons.

See Sally save money, when she buys a Widget. Sally likes to save money. Other people will like to save money on their Widget, too.

See Dick and Jane talk about advertising.

See Dick and Jane prepare an "**advertising plan**".

See Dick and Jane start advertising:

- See Dick and Jane use short phrases.
- See Dick and Jane use words that create "word pictures."
- See Dick and Jane use graphics, photos and cartoons.
- See Dick and Jane remember the **benefits** Widgets offer.

See Dick and Jane's ad get attention.

See Dick and Jane's coupon.

It has a dotted border. Everyone knows it is a coupon.

See the coupon has an expiration date.

See the coupon shows the regular price and the discounted price.

See prospects with dollar signs of savings in their eyes. See customers get excited to save all that money!
See customers run down to buy Widgets.

See Dick and Jane's ad **call the prospect to action.** It says, "Buy today! Call now!"

See Dick and Jane's Yellow Page ad online. See it in the "business to business" section. Widgets are just for business people.

See Dick and Jane commit to advertising as a **"long range goal"**. See Dick and Jane not stop advertising.

See Dick and Jane ask how the customer heard about Widgets.

See Dick and Jane eliminate advertising that doesn't work.

See Dick and Jane increase advertising that works.

See Dick and Jane review their advertising plan annually.

Chapter 13:
See Dick and Jane Learn
to Sell, Sell, Sell

See Jane say, "I can't sell."

See Dick say, "You better learn."

See Dick and Jane disagree.

See Zeke help.

See Zeke ask Jane if she remembers getting an ice cream cone from her daddy after he said, "No." See Jane remember begging..."Please Daddy. Oh, please Daddy. Daddy p-l-e-a-s-e?"

See Zeke show Jane she _is_ a salesman.

See Zeke remind Dick and Jane, "People buy from people they like. People like you because of your good **image**. People know they can **trust** you. Develop **trust** and **credibility**, then they will buy."

See people buy from Jane.

See Zeke remind Jane to **listen**, when she meets people.
"People will tell you how to sell to them, if you listen," says Zeke. "Become <u>genuinely</u> <u>concerned</u> with their <u>needs</u> and develop good <u>interviewing</u> <u>skills</u>."

Zeke says, "Communication is only 5% understood by words and 75% understood in intonation."

See Jane watch her "**manner of presentation**."

People like to deal with people who are like them. See Jane "**match**" her customers. See Jane be an actress.

See Jane determine the **image** her customer perceives. See Jane fit that image. See Jane watch the intonation in her voice.

See Jane have fun matching her customers.

See Zeke tell Jane to learn everything she can about Widgets. Jane must also learn new ways to use Widgets. That will help to sell more Widgets.

See Sally remind Jane to **follow-up** with customers. Customers like to know you care about how their Widget is working for them.
See Sally and Zeke encourage Dick and Jane to go to sales seminars to learn how to sell.

See Dick and Jane learn to "**persuade**" customers to buy Widgets. ("**Persuasion**" is usually not completed until after the third meeting.)

See Dick and Jane persuade customers by:

- Coming **along side** of the customer (like a buddy)

- Creating a **mutual platform** to speak about
- **Telling stories** about what Widgets have done for other customers
- This "**hits hot buttons**"
- See Dick and Jane watching **customer reactions** carefully

See Jane get excited about selling. See Dick say, "This is fun. We just make new friends and help people."

See Dick and Jane learn even more...

See Dick and Jane recognize when the **timing** is right to discuss the sale

See them focus on completing sale without overselling or telling too much.
See Dick and Jane **move the customer to action** by gaining a **timely commitment** See Jane say, "The sale ends tomorrow" or online "click here to learn more."

See Dick and Jane not worry about perfection.

See Dick and Jane get **results!**

See Dick and Jane understand and recognize "**sales resistance.**"

See Earl Nightingale say, "Most people say 'no' because they haven't received <u>enough information</u> yet to say 'yes.'"

See Dick and Jane **make customers feel comfortable.**

See Dick and Jane **desensitize negative** statements and not spend a lot of time on objections.

- See Dick and Jane be polite, but **move on...**
- See Dick and Jane **interrupt** the customer's negative thought cycle.
- See Dick and Jane nicely **distract them** with other information.

See Sally share another special secret.

See Sally tell Dick and Jane about "**high balling and low balling**".

Sally says, "Start with the high price and tell the customer the sale price for 'today only.'"

See the customer get happy about the good price they will pay for their new Widget.

See the customer feel good.

See Dick and Jane feel good selling another Widget...and another!

See Dick and Jane feel good making more money.

Sally says, "Always do what you say you will do and give them more than they expect."
That is called, "**good customer service.**"

Chapter 14:
See Dick and Jane
Provide Customer Service

See Zeke say, "It is easier to maintain an existing client than it is to get a new one!"

Zeke says to send birthday and anniversary cards.

See Dick and Jane be really different.

See Dick and Jane send a birthday card to the customer's Widget.

See their customer think that is so silly that they go buy another Widget for a friend.

See Sally suggest sending thank you cards for everything.

Zeke says, "Stay in touch with your clients at least three times a year. Call them, send to them, drop by their office."

See Dick and Jane make themselves very easy to reach.

See Dick and Jane transfer office calls to their cell phone, when they are away from the office (**out in the field**). (**Note**: Homebased professionals should always say they are "returning to the office" not to their home.)

See Jane use her "**cell phone**" for lots of things besides phone calls. It has calendar. She take notes. She can use apps for everything! Or she can check texts and emails.

See Jane be very available to her customers.

See Dick and Jane "**call in**" for messages **frequently**.

See Dick and Jane get an "**on-hold message**" to tell customers something new about their Widgets, while they wait on-hold.

See Dick and Jane get to their customer quickly. See the customer get off hold.

See Dick and Jane return calls A.S.A.P.

See Zeke remind Dick and Jane that people who need help need it right now. Dick and Jane do not want customers to go to the competition.

See Dick and Jane be "**available**." See Dick and Jane be very available!
See Zeke say that promptly returning calls will make people like them. (Remember, people will buy from you **when they like you**.)

Dick and Jane know that customers cannot come to visit their homebased business. Neighbors don't like the extra traffic.

That is not bad. That is good.

Dick and Jane must take their Widgets to customers. They can meet in a coffee shop. See customers think this is special. This is good customer service.

If you are a homebased professional, good customer service is **very** important. Sally warns them never to make promises they cannot keep.

See Sally remind Dick and Jane to **follow through** with everything they say they will do.
Dick and Jane like their mobile **database app** and their **mobile payment service** app.

See their friendly computer tell them when to do different things for their customers. See it help them provide good follow through.

Dick and Jane have learned that when a customer tells them they are wonderful, they ask them to put it in writing. See Dick and Jane use this in their marketing materials and "**presentation folder**".

See Dick and Jane use "**customer appreciation**" gifts. See them send a special discount certificate to regular customers. See Dick and Jane give them something for referring others to Widgets.

See Dick and Jane **ask** clients what they need.

See Dick and Jane **keep in touch**.

See Dick and Jane ask how they can **improve** their **customer service**.

See Dick and Jane do whatever they must to **meet** their **customer's needs**.
See Dick and Jane give lots of free advice on how to use Widgets.

Chapter 15:
See Dick and Jane Learn Special Homebased Business Secrets

See Sally say, "Homebased businesses are different. Sometimes homebased businesses are very different. Sometimes homebased businesses are just a little different."

See Dick read that now his city requires homebased businesses to be registered. See Dick become a **"registered homebased business"**.

See Dick and Jane do everything the right way. See Dick and Jane act professionally.

See Zeke remind Dick and Jane not to **sound** like a homebased business. See Zeke tell them kids, dogs, birds, television sets, and doorbells are not good business sounds.

See Sally tell Dick and Jane to **educate** friends, family and neighbors about their **professional work status.**

See Zeke say, "Always **appear professional** during work hours in the way you dress and act and even answer your phone."
See Sally remind them that **quality** marketing materials will enhance their **professional image**.

See Zeke tell them to **act bigger** than they are.

See Sally say, "Make isolation your friend. Become **proficient** in the use of the sophisticated equipment now on the market."

See Zeke remind Dick and Jane to keep getting **good press**.

See Sally encourage Dick and Jane to continue **public speaking** so they can become **recognized** Widget **experts** across the country.

See Zeke tell Dick and Jane how important it is to **get out** and **be seen**. He suggests they join more associations.

See Sally remind Dick and Jane to **support others** in business and they will support them. Sally says learning to **give and get referrals** and identify **"referral partners"** is very important.

See Zeke warn Dick and Jane to **know** their **limitations**. He says, "Always do what you say you will do and don't make promises you can't keep."

Finally Sally says, "Offer **superior customer service** and **go the extra mile** for each and every client."

See Zeke and Sally tell Dick and Jane they will sell many Widgets.

See Dick and Jane sell many Widgets.

See Dick and Jane sell Widgets on the **"Internet"**.

See Dick and Jane outgrow their homebased office and open their own Widgets store on Main St.

See Dick and Jane "**franchise**" their Widget stores.

See Dick and Jane's Widget business grow big.

See Dick and Jane's business grow very, very big.

See Dick and Jane make lots of money!